OVERFLOW
Affirmations

DAILY PROPHETIC DECLARATIONS TO POSITION YOU FOR DIVINE OVERFLOW

Published in Sydney, Australia
by Dominion Publishers

First published 2023
This edition published 2023
© 2023 Richard Owusu Amoaye

All rights reserved. No part of this publication may be reproduced, stored in a retrieval system, or transmitted in any form or by any means—for example, electronic, mechanical, photocopy, recording—without the prior written permission of the publisher. The only exception is brief quotations in printed reviews. For licensing/copyright information, for additional copies or for use in specialised settings contact: **info@richardamoayeministries.com**

Emphasis in Scripture highlighted in bold is the author's. Unless otherwise identified, Scripture quotations are from the New King James Version. Copyright ©1982. Used by permission of Thomas Nelson, Inc. All rights reserved. Scripture quotations labeled NIV are from the Holy Bible, New International Version®. NIV®. Copyright © 1973, 1978, 1984 by Biblica, Inc.™ Used by permission of Zondervan. All rights reserved worldwide. www.zondervan.com Scripture quotations labeled AMP are from the Amplified® Bible, Copyright © 1954, 1958, 1962, 1964, 1965, 1987 by The Lockman Foundation. Used by permission.

A catalogue record for this book is available from the National Library of Australia ISBN 978 0 6487581 2 9 (pbk)

Cover designed by **AMK** Designs Australia

Contents

08
Day 1
The Blessedness Of God

10
Day 2
The Beloved Of God

11
Day 3
The Favoured Of God

12
Day 4
The Righteousness Of God

16
Day 5
A Reflection Of The Lord's Goodness

17
Day 6
Humanity: God's Gift To The World

18
Day 7
A Vessel Of Honour

22
Day 8
An Ambassador For Christ

23
Day 9
Faithful

24
Day 10
Joyful

25
Day 11
Patience

30
Day 12
An Overcomer

31
Day 13
Gentle

34
Day 14
Self-Possesion

42
Day 15
Child Of God

43
Day 16
Creative

46
Day 17
Gifted

50
Day 18
A Chosen Generation

51
Day 19
A Royal Priesthood

56
Day 20
Elevated

58
Day 21
An Expression Of God's Wisdom

62
Day 22
An Instrument Of God's Power

63
Day 23
A Carrier Of God's Glory

65
Day 24
A Person Of Value

70
Day 25
A Custodian of the Spirit Empowered Boldness

71
Day 26
An Anointed Vessel Unto The Lord

76
Day 27
A Recepient Of The Peace Of God

77
Day 28
A Beneficiary Of The Light Of God's Countenance

78
Day 29
A Living Temple Of God

80
Day 30
Salt Covenant

BELOVED

One of the many beautiful opportunities we have, yet something that remains underutilised in our day to day walk is our ability to speak and affirm ourselves based on the word of God. To affirm means to openly and publicly 'declare', 'assert', 'proclaim' or 'pronounce'. To do so prophetically means to draw on the word of God and speak its truth over yourself and your circumstances.

As believers, our ability to breakthrough, build and become who God destined us to be depends a lot on two things, our disposition, and the declarations we make. Our lives, experiences, encounters, and testimonies are shaped by our speech; and our speech shaped by what our heart consumes and remains focused on.

When we explore the bible, we learn just how powerful the tongue is and just how measured in our speech we must be. This is because ultimately, and as stated in Proverbs 18:21, " Death and life are in the power of the tongue, and those who love it will eat its fruit". This is why it is important to fill yourself with the word, meditate on it and make biblical declarations over your life and loved ones.

This prophetic affirmations booklet has been designed to help you remain focused on the goodness of God and to concentrate on who He has made you to be. The booklet is inspired by Psalm 45 verse 1 which reads, " My heart is overflowing with a good theme; I recite my composition concerning the King; My tongue is the pen of a ready writer." (NKJV). Each day provides you with scriptures that reflect an aspect of God's goodness, and it provides daily reminders and prompts for you to declare His word.

By focusing on God's word and His goodness, you position your heart to overflow with a good theme. You align yourself to see good, praise Him and testify about who He is.

May this be a blessing to you and may your scripture inspired affirmations propel you to testify!

Calvary Blessings,

Richard Amoaye

DAY 1

The Blessedness Of God

Scriptures For Reflection

Blessed is the man Who walks not in the counsel of the [a]ungodly, Nor stands in the path of sinners, Nor sits in the seat of the scornful; 2 But his delight is in the law of the Lord, And in His law he [b]meditates day and night. 3 He shall be like a tree Planted by the [c]rivers of water, That brings forth its fruit in its season, Whose leaf also shall not wither; And whatever he does shall prosper. **Psalm 1:1-3 NKJV.**

7"Blessed is the man who trusts in the Lord, And whose hope is the Lord. 8For he shall be like a tree planted by the waters, Which spreads out its roots by the river, And will not [c]fear when heat comes; But its leaf will be green, And will not be anxious in the year of drought, Nor will cease from yielding fruit. **Jeremiah 17:7-8 NKJV**

Prayer Points

1. Prayer of thanksgiving for being part of the blessed.
2. Prayer to delight and imbibe the truth of scripture.
3. Declare strength and stability in life is your portion.

Affirmation

I.......... affirm I'm the Blessedness of the Lord. I delight in the word of the Lord, And in the word I will meditate day and night. I'm like a tree Planted by the rivers of water, I will bring forth my fruit in this season, My leaf will be evergreen. I decree and declare I'm prosperous. I'm the Blessedness of the Lord.

DAY 2 THE BELOVED OF GOD

Scripture for Reflection

16 And we have known and believed the love that God has for us. God is love, and he who abides in love abides in God, and God in him. 17 Love has been perfected among us in this: that we may have boldness in the day of judgment; because as He is, so are we in this world. 18 There is no fear in love; but perfect love casts out fear, because fear involves torment. But he who fears has not been made perfect in love. 19 We love [c]Him because He first loved us. **1 John 4:16-19 NKJV.**

12 Therefore, as the elect of God, holy and beloved, put on tender mercies, kindness, humility, meekness, longsuffering; 13 bearing with one another, and forgiving one another, if anyone has a complaint against another; even as Christ forgave you, so you also must do. 14 But above all these things put on love, which is the bond of perfection. 15 And let the peace of God rule in your hearts, to which also you were called in one body; and be thankful. 16 Let the word of Christ dwell in you richly in all wisdom, teaching and admonishing one another in psalms and hymns and spiritual songs, singing with grace in your hearts to the Lord. 17 And whatever you do in word or deed, do all in the name of the Lord Jesus, giving thanks to God the Father through Him. **Colossians 3:12-17 NKJV**

PRAYER POINTS

1. Prayer of thanksgiving for being part of the beloved.
2. Pray for the grace and discipline to abide in the love of God no matter life circumstances.
3. Pray for the grace and wisdom to be a channel of God's love to others.

AFFIRMATION

I............ affirm I'm the Beloved of God. As God Loves me so do I promise to be a channel of His love to others, including those who do not deserve it. I confess from now on, I have been crucified with Christ; and it is no longer I who live, but Christ lives in me; and the life which I now live in the flesh I live by faith in the Son of God, who loved me and gave Himself up for me. I'm the Beloved of God.

The Favoured Of God — DAY 3

Scripture for Reflection

15 Blessed are the people who know the joyful sound! They walk, O Lord, in the light of Your countenance. 16 In Your name they rejoice all day long, And in Your righteousness they are exalted. 17 For You are the glory of their strength, And in Your favor our [c]horn is exalted. 18 For our shield belongs to the Lord, And our king to the Holy One of Israel. **Psalm 89:15-18 NKJV**

My son, do not forget my law, But let your heart keep my commands; 2 For length of days and long life And peace they will add to you. 3 Let not mercy and truth forsake you; Bind them around your neck, Write them on the tablet of your heart, 4 And so find favor and [a]high esteem In the sight of God and man. **Proverbs 3:1-4 NKJV**

Prayer Points

1. Prayer of thanksgiving for being part of the favoured of the Lord.
2. Pray for the grace and discipline to be an instrument of praises to the glorious Lord no matter life circumstances, knowing you are favoured.
3. Decree the favour that releases authority and power on its beneficiaries is your portion.

AFFIRMATION

I......... affirm I'm the favoured of the Lord. In God's name I rejoice all day long, And in His righteousness I have been exalted. For He is the glory of my strength, And in His favour my horn is exalted. The Lord's favour that releases authority and power on its beneficiaries is my portion. I'm the favoured of the Lord

DAY 4
THE RIGHTEOUSNESS OF GOD

Scriptures for Reflection

16 Therefore, from now on, we regard no one according to the flesh. Even though we have known Christ according to the flesh, yet now we know Him thus no longer. 17 Therefore, if anyone is in Christ, he is a new creation; old things have passed away; behold, all things have become new. 18 Now all things are of God, who has reconciled us to Himself through Jesus Christ, and has given us the ministry of reconciliation, 19 that is, that God was in Christ reconciling the world to Himself, not [d] imputing their trespasses to them, and has committed to us the word of reconciliation. 20 Now then, we are ambassadors for Christ, as though God were pleading through us: we implore you on Christ's behalf, be reconciled to God. 21 For He made Him who knew no sin to be sin for us, that we might become the righteousness of God in Him. **2 Corinthians 5:16-21 NKJV**

20 But you have not so learned Christ, 21 if indeed you have heard Him and have been taught by Him, as the truth is in Jesus: 22 that you put off, concerning your former conduct, the old man which grows corrupt according to the deceitful lusts, 23 and be renewed in the spirit of your mind, 24 and that you put on the new man which was created according to God, in true righteousness and holiness. **Ephesians 4:20-24 NKJV**

DAY 4
THE RIGHTEOUSNESS OF GOD

PRAYER POINTS

1. Prayer of Thanksgiving for being part of the Righteousness of God in Christ.
2. Appreciate Jesus Christ for trading places with you.
3. Decree by Christ Jesus and your acceptance of His offered grace, you are right with The Father.

AFFIRMATION

I......... affirm I'm the Righteousness of God in Christ Jesus. Christ has redeemed me from the curse of the Law by becoming a curse for me. For it is written: "Cursed is everyone who is hung on a tree." He took my spot on the cross so I can be right with The Godhead. I am the Righteousness of God in Christ.

> When Jesus spoke again to the people, he said, "I am the light of the world. Whoever follows me will never walk in darkness, but will have the light of life." - John 8:12

DAY 5 A REFLECTION OF THE LORD'S GOODNESS

Scripture for Reflection

For by grace you have been saved through faith, and that not of yourselves; it is the gift of God, 9 not of works, lest anyone should boast. 10 For we are His workmanship, created in Christ Jesus for good works, which God prepared beforehand that we should walk in them. **Ephesians 2:8-10 NKJV.**

16 Do not be deceived, my beloved brethren. 17 Every good gift and every perfect gift is from above, and comes down from the Father of lights, with whom there is no variation or shadow of turning. 18 Of His own will He brought us forth by the word of truth, that we might be a kind of firstfruits of His creatures. **James 1:16-18 NKJV**

PRAYER POINTS

1. Prayer of thanksgiving for being predestined to reflect the Lord's Goodness.
2. Appreciate God for the gift of salvation.
3. Decree by God's grace you will reflect His goodness faithfully.

AFFIRMATION

I......... affirm I'm a Reflection of the Lord's Goodness. I'm saved by grace working through faith. I'm a grateful beneficiary of the gifts of God. His workmanship, created in Christ Jesus for good works, which God prepared beforehand that I should walk in them. I'm a Reflection of the Lord's Goodness.

Humanity
God's Gift To The World

DAY 6

Scripture for Reflection

This is the [a]history of the heavens and the earth when they were created, in the day that the Lord God made the earth and the heavens, 5 before any plant of the field was in the earth and before any herb of the field had grown. For the Lord God had not caused it to rain on the earth, and there was no man to till the ground; 6 but a mist went up from the earth and watered the whole face of the ground. 7 And the Lord God formed man of the dust of the ground, and breathed into his nostrils the breath of life; and man became a living being. **Genesis 2:4-7 NKJV.**

29 The people of the land have used oppressions, committed robbery, and mistreated the poor and needy; and they wrongfully oppress the stranger. 30 So I sought for a man among them who would make a wall, and stand in the gap before Me on behalf of the land, that I should not destroy it; but I found no one. **Ezekiel 22:29-30 NKJV.**

Prayer Points

1. Prayer of thanksgiving for being part of the restored humanity.
2. Appreciate God for creating you in His image.
3. Decree by God's grace you will operate as a restored human.

AFFIRMATION

I......... affirm I'm human. I'm a gift from God to represent His interest on earth. I'm human created in the image and likeness of God to manage the earth on His behalf. I'm human, God's gift to the world.

DAY 7
A Vessel Of Honour

Scripture for Reflection

When I consider Your heavens, the work of Your fingers, The moon and the stars, which You have ordained, What is man that You are mindful of him, And the son of man that You visit[c] him? For You have made him a little lower than [d]the angels, And You have crowned him with glory and honor. You have made him to have dominion over the works of Your hands; You have put all things under his feet, All sheep and oxen— Even the beasts of the field, The birds of the air, And the fish of the sea That pass through the paths of the seas. **Psalm 8:3-8 NKJV**.

Prayer Points

1. Prayer of thanksgiving for being a vessel of honour.
2. Purge yourself from any thought, speech and actions that defile and undermine you and your usefulness in the Kingdom.
3. Decree by God's grace you will operate as an instrument of Honour.

Affirmation

I......... affirm I'm a Vessel of Honour. My God has crowned me with glory and honour. He created me to have dominion over the works of His hands; He has put all things under my feet. I'm a Vessel of Honour.

PART 2
OVERFLOW
Affirmations
DAILY PROPHETIC DECLARATIONS TO POSITION YOU FOR DIVINE OVERFLOW

DAY 8 An Ambassador For Christ

Scripture for Reflection

18 Now all things are of God, who has reconciled us to Himself through Jesus Christ, and has given us the ministry of reconciliation, 19 that is, that God was in Christ reconciling the world to Himself, not [a]imputing their trespasses to them, and has committed to us the word of reconciliation 20 Now then, we are ambassadors for Christ, as though God were pleading through us: we implore you on Christ's behalf, be reconciled to God. 21 For He made Him who knew no sin to be sin for us, that we might become the righteousness of God in Him. **2 Corinthians 5:18-21 NKJV**.

...and for me, that utterance may be given to me, that I may open my mouth boldly to make known the mystery of the gospel, 20 for which I am an ambassador in chains; that in it I may speak boldly, as I ought to speak. **Ephesians 6:19-20 NKJV**

PRAYER POINTS

1. Prayer of thanksgiving for being part of the ambassadors for Christ.
2. Gratitude to God for reconciling us to Himself through Jesus.
3. Decree by God's grace you will operate as a faithful ambassador, worthy of the high calling

AFFIRMATION

I......... affirm I'm an Ambassador for Christ. God through Christ reconciled me to Himself, not imputing my trespasses to me, and has committed to me the word of reconciliation. Now then, I'm an ambassador for Christ. On Christ's behalf, I seek to reconcile others to God through Christ. For God made Christ who knew no sin to be sin for me, that I might become the righteousness of God in Him. I'm an Ambassador for Christ.

DAY 9 — FAITHFUL

Scripture for Reflection

Paul, an apostle of Christ Jesus by the will of God, To God's holy people in Ephesus, the faithful in Christ Jesus: Ephesians 1:1

8 "And to the [d]angel of the church in Smyrna write,'These things says the First and the Last, who was dead, and came to life: 9 "I know your works, tribulation, and poverty (but you are rich); and I know the blasphemy of those who say they are Jews and are not, but are a [e]synagogue of Satan. 10 Do not fear any of those things which you are about to suffer. Indeed, the devil is about to throw some of you into prison, that you may be tested, and you will have tribulation ten days. Be faithful until death, and I will give you the crown of life. 11 "He who has an ear, let him hear what the Spirit says to the churches. He who overcomes shall not be hurt by the second death."'. Revelation 2:8-11 NKJV.

1 This, then, is how you ought to regard us: as servants of Christ and as those entrusted with the mysteries God has revealed. 2 Now it is required that those who have been given a trust must prove faithful. 1 Corinthians 4:1-2 NKJV

PRAYER POINTS

1. Prayer of thanksgiving for being part of the Faithful.
2. Gratitude to God for entrusting us with the Kingdom message.
3. Decree by God's grace you will operate as a faithful servant, worthy of the high calling.

AFFIRMATION

I......... affirm I'm Faithful. I do not fear the machinations and persecution from godless beings. I access the grace to be resolute in spreading the good news no matter the opposition. I declare I'm faithful until THE END. I intend to receive my promised crown of life. I'm Faithful.

DAY 10
JOYFUL

Scripture for Reflection

2 My brethren, count it all joy when you fall into various trials, 3 knowing that the testing of your faith produces patience. **James 1:2-3 NKJV.**

Therefore, since we have been justified by faith, we[a] have peace with God through our Lord Jesus Christ. 2 Through him we have also obtained access by faith[b] into this grace in which we stand, and we[c] rejoice[d] in hope of the glory of God. 3 Not only that, but we rejoice in our sufferings, knowing that suffering produces endurance, 4 and endurance produces character, and character produces hope, 5 and hope does not put us to shame, because God's love has been poured into our hearts through the Holy Spirit who has been given to us.
Romans 5:1-5 ESV

You will show me the path of life; In Your presence is fullness of joy; At Your right hand are pleasures forevermore. **Psalm 16:11 NKJV**

8 Though you have not seen him, you love him; and even though you do not see him now, you believe in him and are filled with an inexpressible and glorious joy, 9 for you are receiving the end result of your faith, the salvation of your souls. **1 Peter 1:8-9 NIV.**

PRAYER POINTS

1. Prayer of thanksgiving for being part of the Joyful.
2. Gratitude to God for entrusting us with His Presence.
3. Decree by God's grace you are filled with an inexpressible and glorious joy.

AFFIRMATION

I......... affirm I'm Joyful. Thank you Jesus for you have acquitted me of my sin, and declared me blameless before God. I'm Joyful for I have peace with God through my Lord and Saviour Jesus Christ . Through Him I also have access by faith into this [remarkable state of] grace in which I [firmly and safely and securely] stand. I rejoice in my [a]hope and the confident assurance of [experiencing and enjoying] the glory of [my great] God [the manifestation of His excellence and power] And not only this, but [with joy] I delight in sufferings and rejoice in my hardships, knowing that hardship (distress, pressure, trouble) produces patient endurance. I'm Joyful

PATIENCE — DAY 11

Scripture for Reflection

11 And Samuel said, "What have you done?" And Saul said, "When I saw that the people were scattered from me, and that you did not come within the days appointed, and that the Philistines gathered together at Michmash, 12 then I said, 'The Philistines will now come down on me at Gilgal, and I have not made supplication to the Lord.' Therefore I felt compelled, and offered a burnt offering." 13 And Samuel said to Saul, "You have done foolishly. You have not kept the commandment of the Lord your God, which He commanded you. For now the Lord would have established your kingdom over Israel forever. **1 Samuel 13:11-13 NKJV**

7 Therefore be patient, brethren, until the coming of the Lord. See how the farmer waits for the precious fruit of the earth, waiting patiently for it until it receives the early and latter rain. 8 You also be patient. Establish your hearts, for the coming of the Lord [f]is at hand. 9 Do not [g]grumble against one another, brethren, lest you be [h]condemned. Behold, the Judge is standing at the door! 10 My brethren, take the prophets, who spoke in the name of the Lord, as an example of suffering and patience. 11 Indeed we count them blessed who endure. You have heard of the perseverance of Job and seen the end intended by the Lord—that the Lord is very compassionate and merciful. **James 5:7-11 NKJV**

Prayer Points

12 Therefore, as the elect of God, holy and beloved, put on tender mercies, kindness, humility, meekness, longsuffering; 13 bearing with one another, and forgiving one another, if anyone has a complaint against another; even as Christ forgave you, so you also must do. **Colossians 3:12-13 NKJV**.

1. Ask the Lord for the power to renew your patience and strength. And above all things have fervent love for one another, for "love will cover a multitude of sins." Be hospitable to one another without grumbling. **1 Peter 4:8-9 NKJV**

2. Thank God for giving you patience to be kind and compassionate when you don't have your own and for loving you when You are the one who's difficult in someone else's life.

DAY 11: Patience

" Be anxious for nothing, but in everything by prayer and supplication, with thanksgiving, let your requests be made known to God; 7 and the peace of God, which surpasses all understanding, will guard your hearts and minds through Christ Jesus. Philippians 4:6-7 NKJV

3. Ask God for the grace to carry you through crises.

AFFIRMATION

I......... affirm I'm patient. I declare I have access to patience to stand the test of time until the coming of the Lord. My heart is established in God's wisdom. I declare by the grace of God I will not grumble against my neighbour. I pronounce from today I will hunger for the plans and will of God for my life. By the sovereign will of God I have been given the patience to linger in God's presence. Oh Lord thank you for pausing my racing thoughts and self-imposed time limits. Thank you for being the only one who can truly take away my urge to do life by myself. Thank you for showing me that putting you first is what's best for me. I affirm with all my strength I am patient.

29

DAY 12 AN OVERCOMER

Scripture for Reflection

Whoever believes that Jesus is the Christ is born of God, and everyone who loves Him who begot also loves him who is begotten of Him. 2 By this we know that we love the children of God, when we love God and keep His commandments. 3 For this is the love of God, that we keep His commandments. And His commandments are not burdensome. 4 For whatever is born of God overcomes the world. And this is the victory that has overcome the world—[a] our faith. 5 Who is he who overcomes the world, but he who believes that Jesus is the Son of God? 1 John 5:1-5 NKJV.

4 You are of God, little children, and have overcome them, because He who is in you is greater than he who is in the world. 5 They are of the world. Therefore they speak as of the world, and the world hears them.   1 John 4:4-5 NKJV.
32 Indeed the hour is coming, yes, has now come, that you will be scattered, each to his [e] own, and will leave Me alone. And yet I am not alone, because the Father is with Me. 33 These things I have spoken to you, that in Me you may have peace. In the world you [f]will have tribulation; but be of good cheer, I have overcome the world." John 16:32-33 NKJV

PRAYER POINTS

1. Prayer of thanksgiving for being part of those who believes in the Lordship of Jesus.
2. Pray for the grace to continue to love God and keep His commandments.
3. Decree by God's grace you are an Overcomer.

AFFIRMATION

I......... affirm I'm an Overcomer. I believe that Jesus is the Christ and He is born of God, I love Him, and love those who are begotten of Him. I confess because He lives I can face tomorrow confidently. I know I'm born of God and therefore an overcomer of the world. According to the word of God, my faith in Jesus Christ is the victory that has overcome the world. I declare by the grace of God and the finished work of the Cross no weapon fashioned against me and my family will prevail. I affirm with the weapon of The Word, The Name and The Blood no power stands a chance against me, for according to the Word, we overcome the Devil and his cohorts by the Blood of the Lamb and by the testimony of our witness. I am an Overcomer.

DAY 13
GENTLE

Scripture for Reflection

1 Therefore, my beloved and longed-for brethren, my joy and crown, so stand fast in the Lord, beloved. 2 I implore Euodia and I implore Syntyche to be of the same mind in the Lord. 3 And I urge you also, true companion, help these women who labored with me in the gospel, with Clement also, and the rest of my fellow workers, whose names are in the Book of Life. 4 Rejoice in the Lord always. Again I will say, rejoice! 5 Let your gentleness be known to all men. the Lord is at hand. **Philippians 4:1-5 NKJV.**

12 Therefore, as God's chosen people, holy and dearly loved, clothe yourselves with compassion, kindness, humility, gentleness and patience. 13 Bear with each other and forgive one another if any of you has a grievance against someone. Forgive as the Lord forgave you. 14 And over all these virtues put on love, which binds them all together in perfect unity. 15 Let the peace of Christ rule in your hearts, since as members of one body you were called to peace. And be thankful. **Colossians 3:12-15 NKJV.**

28 "Come to me, all you who are weary and burdened, and I will give you rest. 29 Take my yoke upon you and learn from me, for I am gentle and humble in heart, and you will find rest for your souls. 30 For my yoke is easy and my burden is light." **Matthew 11:28-30 NKJV.**

PRAYER POINTS

1 He tends his flock like a shepherd: He gathers the lambs in his arms and carries them close to his heart; he gently leads those that have young. **Isaiah 40:11.**

1. Thank Jesus for being considerate in disposition towards you. "By the humility and gentleness of Christ, I appeal to you—I, Paul, who am "timid" when face to face with you, but "bold" toward you when away! 2 I beg you that when I come I may not have to be as bold as I expect to be toward some people who think that we live by the standards of this world". **2 Corinthians 10:1-2.**
2. Pray for the grace to model the humility and gentleness of Christ.
3. Decree by God's grace you are Gentle.

DAY 13: Gentle

AFFIRMATION

I......... affirm I'm Gentle. Master Jesus help me to continue to come to terms with my own selfishness and ignorance. Help me accept my own frailty that I'm needy and broken and realize that, if I were not, I would be like God. I decree gentleness toward myself and others from this day forward. I decree I will not substitute material things for love or for gentleness or for tenderness or for a sense of good fellowship. Master Jesus thank you for helping me to understand money, power, and fame is not the ultimate sign of your blessing but Love, Joy, Peace, Patience, Kindness, Goodness, Faithfulness, GENTLENESS and Self-Control. I affirm I am Gentle.

DAY 14
SELF-POSSESSION

Scripture for Reflection

14 We know that the law is spiritual; but I am unspiritual, sold as a slave to sin. 15 I do not understand what I do. For what I want to do I do not do, but what I hate I do. 16 And if I do what I do not want to do, I agree that the law is good. 17 As it is, it is no longer I myself who do it, but it is sin living in me. 18 For I know that good itself does not dwell in me, that is, in my sinful nature.[c] For I have the desire to do what is good, but I cannot carry it out. 19 For I do not do the good I want to do, but the evil I do not want to do—this I keep on doing. 20 Now if I do what I do not want to do, it is no longer I who do it, but it is sin living in me that does it. **Romans 7:14-20**

24 What a wretched man I am! Who will rescue me from this body that is subject to death? 25 Thanks be to God, who delivers me through Jesus Christ our Lord! **Romans 7:24-25**

Doing Good for the Sake of the Gospel

1 You, however, must teach what is appropriate to sound doctrine. 2 Teach the older men to be temperate, worthy of respect, self-controlled, and sound in faith, in love and in endurance. 3 Likewise, teach the older women to be reverent in the way they live, not to be slanderers or addicted to much wine, but to teach what is good. 4 Then they can urge the younger women to love their husbands and children, 5 to be self-controlled and pure, to be busy at home, to be kind, and to be subject to their husbands, so that no one will malign the word of God. 6 Similarly, encourage the young men to be self-controlled. 7 In everything set them an example by doing what is good. In your teaching show integrity, seriousness 8 and soundness of speech that cannot be condemned, so that those who oppose you may be ashamed because they have nothing bad to say about us. 9 Teach slaves to be subject to their masters in everything, to try to please them, not to talk back to them, 10 and not to steal

Self-Possession — Day 14

from them, but to show that they can be fully trusted, so that in every way they will make the teaching about God our Savior attractive. 11 For the grace of God has appeared that offers salvation to all people. 12 It teaches us to say "No" to ungodliness and worldly passions, and to live self-controlled, upright and godly lives in this present age, 13 while we wait for the blessed hope—the appearing of the glory of our great God and Savior, Jesus Christ, 14 who gave himself for us to redeem us from all wickedness and to purify for himself a people that are his very own, eager to do what is good. 15 These, then, are the things you should teach. Encourage and rebuke with all authority. Do not let anyone despise you. **Titus 2 NIV**.

1 Simon Peter, a servant and apostle of Jesus Christ, To those who through the righteousness of our God and Savior Jesus Christ have received a faith as precious as ours: 2 Grace and peace be yours in abundance through the knowledge of God and of Jesus our Lord. Confirming One's Calling and Election. 3 His divine power has given us everything we need for a godly life through our knowledge of him who called us by his own glory and goodness. 4 Through these he has given us his very great and precious promises, so that through them you may participate in the divine nature, having escaped the corruption in the world caused by evil desires. 5 For this very reason, make every effort to add to your faith goodness; and to goodness, knowledge; 6 and to knowledge, self-control; and to self-control, perseverance; and to perseverance, godliness; 7 and to godliness, mutual affection; and to mutual affection, love. 8 For if you possess these qualities in increasing measure, they will keep you from being ineffective and unproductive in your knowledge of our Lord Jesus Christ. 9 But whoever does not have them is nearsighted and blind, forgetting that they have been cleansed from their past sins. 10 Therefore, my brothers and sisters,[a] make every effort to confirm your calling and election. For if you do these things, you will never stumble, 11 and you will receive a rich welcome into the eternal kingdom of our Lord and Savior Jesus Christ. **2 Peter 1:1-11 NIV. (5-8)**

DAY 14
SELF-POSSESSION

PRAYER POINTS

1. Thank God, for your deliverance from the law of sin in the flesh through Jesus Christ your Lord.
2. Thank God for His grace that has appeared that offers salvation and teaches us to say "No" to ungodliness and worldly passions, and to live self-controlled, upright and godly lives in this present evil age.
3. Decree by God's grace you possess all your faculties.

AFFIRMATION

I.......... affirm I Possess Myself. My Lord, Jesus Christ's divine power has given me everything I need for a godly life through my knowledge of him who called me by his own glory and goodness. Through this He has given me these very great and precious promises, so that through them I may participate in the divine nature, having escaped the corruption in the world caused by evil desires. For this very reason, I make ever effort to add to my faith, goodness; and to goodness, knowledge; and to knowledge, self-control and to self-control, perseverance; and to perseverance, godliness; and to godliness, mutual affection; and to mutual affection, love. Through the inner working of the Holy Spirit, I affirm, I possess myself.

PART 3

OVERFLOW

Affirmations

DAILY PROPHETIC DECLARATIONS TO POSITION YOU FOR DIVINE OVERFLOW

DAY 15
CHILD OF GOD

Scriptures for Reflection

10 He was in the world, and the world was made through Him, and the world did not know Him. 11 He came to His [c]own, and His [d]own did not receive Him. 12 But as many as received Him, to them He gave the [e]right to become children of God, to those who believe in His name: 13 who were born, not of blood, nor of the will of the flesh, nor of the will of man, but of God. **John 1:10-13 NKJV**

26 For you are all sons of God through faith in Christ Jesus. 27 For as many of you as were baptized into Christ have put on Christ. 28 There is neither Jew nor Greek, there is neither slave nor free, there is neither male nor female; for you are all one in Christ Jesus. 29 And if you are Christ's, then you are Abraham's seed, and heirs according to the promise. **Galatians 3:26-29 NKJV**

14 For as many as are led by the Spirit of God, these are sons of God. 15 For you did not receive the spirit of bondage again to fear, but you received the Spirit of adoption by whom we cry out, "Abba,[e] Father." 16 The Spirit Himself bears witness with our spirit that we are children of God, 17 and if children, then heirs—heirs of God and joint heirs with Christ, if indeed we suffer with Him, that we may also be glorified together. **Romans 8:14-17 NKJV**

PRAYER POINTS

1. Prayer of thanksgiving for being a Child of God.
2. Pray for the grace and wisdom to be sensitive to the leading and prompting of the Spirit.
3. Decree by God's grace you are a Child of God.

AFFIRMATION

I……… affirm I'm a Child of God. I am a child of God through faith in Christ Jesus. I am born, not of blood, nor of the will of the flesh, nor of the will of man, but the will of God. For I have been baptised into Christ and I have put on Christ. And if I'm Christ's, then I am Abraham's seed, and an heir according to the promise. As I am led by the Spirit of God, I am a Child of God. I have not received the spirit of bondage, but I received the Spirit of adoption by whom I cry out, "Abba, Father." The Holy Spirit Himself bears witness with my spirit that I am a Child of God, and if I am a Child of God then an heir of God and joint heirs with Christ. I am a Child of God.

DAY 16 CREATIVE

Scriptures for Reflection

Then the Lord spoke to Moses, saying: 2 "See, I have called by name Bezalel the son of Uri, the son of Hur, of the tribe of Judah. 3 And I have filled him with the Spirit of God, in wisdom, in understanding, in knowledge, and in all manner of workmanship, 4 to design artistic works, to work in gold, in silver, in bronze, 5 in cutting jewels for setting, in carving wood, and to work in all manner of workmanship. 6 "And I, indeed I, have appointed with him Aholiab the son of Ahisamach, of the tribe of Dan; and I have put wisdom in the hearts of all the gifted artisans, that they may make all that I have commanded you: **Exodus 31:1-6**

30 And Moses said to the children of Israel, "See, the Lord has called by name Bezalel the son of Uri, the son of Hur, of the tribe of Judah; 31 and He has filled him with the Spirit of God, in wisdom and understanding, in knowledge and all manner of workmanship, 32 to design artistic works, to work in gold and silver and bronze, 33 in cutting jewels for setting, in carving wood, and to work in all manner of artistic workmanship. 34 "And He has put in his heart the ability to teach, in him and Aholiab the son of Ahisamach, of the tribe of Dan. 35 He has filled them with skill to do all manner of work of the engraver and the designer and the tapestry maker, in blue, purple, and scarlet thread, and fine linen, and of the weaver—those who do every work and those who design artistic works. **Exodus 35:30-35 NKJV**

Do you see a man who [h]excels in his work? He will stand before kings; He will not stand before [i]unknown men. Proverbs 22:29 NKJV 10 For we are His workmanship [His own master work, a work of art], created in Christ Jesus [reborn from above—spiritually transformed, renewed, ready to be used] for good works, which God prepared [for us] beforehand [taking paths which He set], so that we would walk in them [living the good life which He prearranged and made ready for us]. **Ephesians 2:10 AMP**

23 Whatever you do [whatever your task may be], work from the soul [that is, put in your very best effort], as [something done] for the Lord and not for men, 24 knowing [with all certainty] that it is from the Lord [not from men] that you will receive the inheritance which is your [greatest] reward. It is the Lord Christ whom you [actually] serve. **Colossians 3:23-24 AMP**

DAY 16
CREATIVE

PRAYER POINTS

1. Prayer of thanksgiving for being created in the image of God.
2. Pray for the grace and wisdom to be diligent and faithful in your work.
3. Decree by God's grace you are a Creative.

AFFIRMATION

I……… affirm I'm Creative. As a Child of God, He made me in His image. I am a masterpiece of the ultimate Creator. Since I am made in His image I possess the communicable essence that lives in that image: Love, Patience, Kindness, Self-Possession and of course CREATIVITY! I totally and whole heartedly embrace the fact I have been crafted in God's image today and accept His permission for me to be the artist/inventor/innovator/creative genius He made me to be. I decree with all diligence I will be a good steward with the spirit of creativity God has given me. I decree in the mighty name of Jesus, my products and services will bring healing, restoration and man to the saving grace. I am Creative.

DAY 17
GIFTED

Scriptures for Reflection

10 As each one has received a gift, minister it to one another, as good stewards of the manifold grace of God. 11 If anyone speaks, let him speak as the [c]oracles of God. If anyone ministers, let him do it as with the ability which God supplies, that in all things God may be glorified through Jesus Christ, to whom belong the glory and the [d]dominion forever and ever. Amen. 1 **Peter 4:10-11 NKJV**.

Now concerning spiritual gifts, brethren, I do not want you to be ignorant: 2 You know that[a] you were Gentiles, carried away to these dumb[b] idols, however you were led. 3 Therefore I make known to you that no one speaking by the Spirit of God calls Jesus [c]accursed, and no one can say that Jesus is Lord except by the Holy Spirit. 4 There are [d]diversities of gifts, but the same Spirit. 5 There are differences of ministries, but the same Lord. 6 And there are diversities of activities, but it is the same God who works [e]all in all. 7 But the manifestation of the Spirit is given to each one for the profit of all: 8 for to one is given the word of wisdom through the Spirit, to another the word of knowledge through the same Spirit, 9 to another faith by the same Spirit, to another gifts of healings by [f]the same Spirit, 10 to another the working of miracles, to another prophecy, to another discerning of spirits, to another different kinds of tongues, to another the interpretation of tongues. 11 But one and the same Spirit works all these things, distributing to each one individually as He wills.**1 Corinthians 12:1-11 NKJV.**

Living Sacrifices to God

12 I beseech[a] you therefore, brethren, by the mercies of God, that you present your bodies a living sacrifice, holy, acceptable to God, which is your [b]reasonable service. 2 And do not be conformed to this world, but be transformed by the renewing of your mind, that you may prove what is that good and acceptable and perfect will of God.

DAY 17
Gifted

Serve God with Spiritual Gifts

3 For I say, through the grace given to me, to everyone who is among you, not to think of himself more highly than he ought to think, but to think soberly, as God has dealt to each one a measure of faith. 4 For as we have many members in one body, but all the members do not have the same function, 5 so we, being many, are one body in Christ, and individually members of one another. 6 Having then gifts differing according to the grace that is given to us, let us use them: if prophecy, let us prophesy in proportion to our faith; 7 or ministry, let us use it in our ministering; he who teaches, in teaching; 8 he who exhorts, in exhortation; he who gives, with liberality; he who leads, with diligence; he who shows mercy, with cheerfulness.

Behave Like a Christian

9 Let love be without hypocrisy. Abhor what is evil. Cling to what is good. 10 Be kindly affectionate to one another with brotherly love, in honor giving preference to one another; 11 not lagging in diligence, fervent in spirit, serving the Lord; 12 rejoicing in hope, patient[c] in tribulation, continuing steadfastly in prayer; 13 distributing to the needs of the saints, given[d] to hospitality. 14 Bless those who persecute you; bless and do not curse. 15 Rejoice with those who rejoice, and weep with those who weep. 16 Be of the same mind toward one another. Do not set your mind on high things, but associate with the humble. Do not be wise in your own opinion. 17 Repay no one evil for evil. Have[e] regard for good things in the sight of all men. 18 If it is possible, as much as depends on you, live peaceably with all men. 19 Beloved, do not avenge yourselves, but rather give place to wrath; for it is written, "Vengeance is Mine, I will repay," says the Lord. 20 Therefore "If your enemy is hungry, feed him; If he is thirsty, give him a drink; For in so doing you will heap coals of fire on his head." 21 Do not be overcome by evil, but overcome evil with good. **Romans 12 NKJV.**

DAY 17
GIFTED

PRAYER POINTS

1. Prayer of thanksgiving for being Gifted.
2. Pray for the grace and wisdom to be diligent and faithful in using your gift for the benefit of others.
3. Decree by God's grace you are gifted

AFFIRMATION

I......... affirm I am Gifted. As a gifted gift, I will practice hospitality without complaint. I acknowledge God has graciously gifted others near and far with special abilities as well for mutual benefits. Thank you my Lord God for gifting each person with a unique set of abilities and talents. I commit to the full discovery of all my gifting, abilities and talents, and to develop them with time and experience if need be. I avail myself Lord, equip me to accomplish Your love on earth by using my gifts to bless others. From this day onwards It is a privilege to be part of God's plan. I decree there is space and opportunity to use my gifts to benefit society and my world. I acknowledge I have been endowed with spiritual gifts as well for the common good of the body of Christ. Thank you God the Holy Spirit for trusting me. I am Gifted.

DAY 18
A Chosen Generation

Scriptures for Reflection

But you are a chosen generation, a royal priesthood, a holy nation, His own special people, that you may proclaim the praises of Him who called you out of darkness into His marvelous light; 10 who once were not a people but are now the people of God, who had not obtained mercy but now have obtained mercy. **1 Peter 2:9-10 NKJV.**

Hear me when I call, O God of my righteousness! You have relieved me in my distress; [b]Have mercy on me, and hear my prayer. 2 How long, O you sons of men, Will you turn my glory to shame? How long will you love worthlessness And seek falsehood? Selah 3 But know that the Lord has [c] set apart for Himself him who is godly; the Lord will hear when I call to Him. **Psalm 4:1-3 NKJV.**

Praise the Lord! Praise the name of the Lord; Praise Him, O you servants of the Lord! 2 You who stand in the house of the Lord, In the courts of the house of our God, 3 Praise the Lord, for the Lord is good; Sing praises to His name, for it is pleasant. 4 For the Lord has chosen Jacob for Himself, Israel for His [a]special treasure. **Psalm 135:1-4 NKJV.**

PRAYER POINTS

1. Prayer of thanksgiving for being Among the Chosen Generation.
2. Pray for insight and appreciation of what it means to be Chosen to proclaim the praises of Him who called us in Himself before time.
3. Decree by God's grace you are a Chosen Generation

AFFIRMATION

I……… affirm I am a Chosen Generation. I have been called forth to show the excellence of my God. All I require and will ever require for life, God has given me freely, I know who I am. I am a chosen generation, I have been called to show forth the might of my God. All I require for life, God has given me in Christ Jesus and boldly I confess I know whose I am. I know who God says I am. I know what He says I am. I know where He says I am at. I am working in power, I am working miracles, I live a life of favour, for I know who I am. I am a chosen generation, a royal priesthood, a holy nation, His own special image, I have been empowered to proclaim the praises of my God and my Father who called me out of darkness into His marvelous light. Once I did not belong but now I am a covenant Child of His Majesty. Yes I know who and whose I am. I affirm confidently, I am a Chosen Generation!

A Royal Priesthood

DAY 19

Scriptures for Reflection

Our Inheritance Through Christ's Blood

Therefore, laying aside all malice, all deceit, hypocrisy, envy, and all evil speaking, 2 as newborn babes, desire the pure milk of the word, that you may grow [a]thereby, 3 if indeed you have tasted that the Lord is gracious.

The Chosen Stone and His Chosen People

4 Coming to Him as to a living stone, rejected indeed by men, but chosen by God and precious, 5 you also, as living stones, are being built up a spiritual house, a holy priesthood, to offer up spiritual sacrifices acceptable to God through Jesus Christ. 6 Therefore it is also contained in the Scripture, "Behold, I lay in Zion A chief cornerstone, elect, precious, And he who believes on Him will by no means be put to shame." 7 Therefore, to you who believe, He is precious; but to those who [b]are disobedient, "The stone which the builders rejected Has become the chief cornerstone," 8 and "A stone of stumbling And a rock of offense." They stumble, being disobedient to the word, to which they also were appointed. 9 But you are a chosen generation, a royal priesthood, a holy nation, His own special people, that you may proclaim the praises of Him who called you out of darkness into His marvelous light; 10 who once were not a people but are now the people of God, who had not obtained mercy but now have obtained mercy. **1 Peter 2:1-10 NKJV**

The author of the Book of Hebrews is writing about two different kinds of priests. There were the priests who came from the tribe (family) of Levi (Hebrews 7:5). And there was Melchizedek, who was a different kind of priest (Hebrews 7:6). Most modern readers would only know about the first of these. Israel's priests all came from the family of Aaron, which was part of the tribe of Levi. Other members of the tribe of Levi (called Levites) assisted them in their duties. God told Moses to establish these priests. And the first priests were Moses' brother Aaron, and his sons. Afterwards, all Israel's priests came from that family. Some famous priests include Ezekiel, Eli, Annas and Caiaphas. Zechariah and his son John (usually called John the Baptist) also belonged to this family.

DAY 19
A ROYAL PRIESTHOOD
PRAYER POINTS

1. Prayer of thanksgiving for being A Royal Priesthood.

2. Pray for insight and appreciation of what it means to be A Royal Priesthood, chosen to offer up spiritual sacrifices acceptable to God through Jesus Christ.

3. Decree by God's grace you are a Royal Priesthood!

AFFIRMATION

I......... affirm I am A Royal Priesthood. I have been chosen to offer up spiritual sacrifices, acceptable to God through Jesus Christ. I am a holy priest unto God, therefore my body is offered as a living sacrifice, holy and pleasing to my God – this is my spiritual act of worship. As A Royal Priesthood, I will continually offer the sacrifice of praise to my God, that is, the fruit of my lips, giving thanks to His glorious name. I will not forget to do good and to share with others, for I know as A Priest my God is pleased with such sacrifices. I affirm, I am A Royal Priesthood.

DAY 20
ELEVATED

Scriptures for Reflection

We give thanks to You, O God, we give thanks! For Your wondrous works declare that Your name is near. 2 "When I choose the [b]proper time, I will judge uprightly. 3 The earth and all its inhabitants are dissolved; I set up its pillars firmly. Selah 4 "I said to the boastful, 'Do not deal boastfully,' And to the wicked, 'Do not [c]lift up the horn. 5 Do not lift up your horn on high; Do not speak with [d]a stiff neck.'" 6 For exaltation comes neither from the east Nor from the west nor from the south 7 But God is the Judge: He puts down one, And exalts another. 8 For in the hand of the Lord there is a cup, And the wine is red; It is fully mixed, and He pours it out; Surely its dregs shall all the wicked of the earth Drain and drink down. 9 But I will declare forever, I will sing praises to the God of Jacob. 10 "All the [e]horns of the wicked I will also cut off, But the horns of the righteous shall be exalted." **Psalm 75 NKJV**

46 Then King Nebuchadnezzar fell on his face, prostrate before Daniel, and commanded that they should present an offering and incense to him. 47 The king answered Daniel, and said, "Truly your God is the God of gods, the Lord of kings, and a revealer of secrets, since you could reveal this secret." 48 Then the king promoted Daniel and gave him many great gifts; and he made him ruler over the whole province of Babylon, and chief administrator over all the wise men of Babylon. 49 Also Daniel petitioned the king, and he set Shadrach, Meshach, and Abed-Nego over the affairs of the province of Babylon; but Daniel sat in [p]the gate of the king. **Daniel 2:46-49 NKJV**.

5 Likewise you younger people, submit yourselves to your elders. Yes, all of you be submissive to one another, and be clothed with humility, for "God resists the proud, But gives grace to the humble." 6 Therefore humble yourselves under the mighty hand of God, that He may exalt you in due time, **1 Peter 5:5-6 NKJV**.

DAY 20
ELEVATED

12 the Lord will open to you His good [c]treasure, the heavens, to give the rain to your land in its season, and to bless all the work of your hand. You shall lend to many nations, but you shall not borrow. 13 And the Lord will make you the head and not the tail; you shall be above only, and not be beneath, if you [d]heed the commandments of the Lord your God, which I command you today, and are careful to observe them. **Deuteronomy 28:12-14 NKJV**.

PRAYER POINTS

1. Prayer of thanksgiving for being part of the Elevated.
2. Pray for insight and appreciation of why the Lord Elevated you.
3. Decree by God's grace you are Elevated!

AFFIRMATION

I......... affirm, I am Elevated. The Lord has opened to me His good treasure. The heavens have given rain to my land in its season, and to bless all the work of my hand. I shall lend to many nations; my name is deleted from the list of borrowers. I decree my Lord has made me the head and not the tail; I am above and Elevated in honour only, and not beneath and dejected. I have set the Lord before me. As the righteousness of my God, my horns shall continuously be exalted. I affirm, I am Elevated!

DAY 21
AN EXPRESSION OF GOD'S WISDOM

Scriptures for Reflection

2 My brethren, count it all joy when you fall into various trials, 3 knowing that the testing of your faith produces [a]patience. 4 But let patience have its perfect work, that you may be [b]perfect and complete, lacking nothing. 5 If any of you lacks wisdom, let him ask of God, who gives to all liberally and without reproach, and it will be given to him. 6 But let him ask in faith, with no doubting, for he who doubts is like a wave of the sea driven and tossed by the wind. 7 For let not that man suppose that he will receive anything from the Lord; 8 he is a double-minded man, unstable in all his ways. **James 1:2-8 NKJV**.

13 Who among you is wise and intelligent? Let him by his good conduct show his [good] deeds with the gentleness and humility of true wisdom. 14 But if you have bitter jealousy and selfish ambition in your hearts, do not be arrogant, and [as a result] be in defiance of the truth. 15 This [superficial] wisdom is not that which comes down from above, but is earthly (secular), natural (unspiritual), even demonic. 16 For where jealousy and selfish ambition exist, there is disorder [unrest, rebellion] and every evil thing and morally degrading practice. 17 But the wisdom from above is first pure [morally and spiritually undefiled], then peace-loving [courteous, considerate], gentle, reasonable [and willing to listen], full of compassion and good fruits. It is unwavering, without [self-righteous] hypocrisy [and self-serving guile]. 18 And the seed whose fruit is righteousness (spiritual maturity) is sown in peace by those who make peace [by actively encouraging goodwill between individuals]. **James 3:13-18 AMP**

My son, if you receive my words, And treasure my commands within you, 2 So that you incline your ear to wisdom, And apply your heart to understanding; 3 Yes, if you cry out for discernment, And lift up your voice for understanding, 4 If you seek her as silver, And search for her as for hidden treasures; 5 Then you will understand the fear of the Lord, And find the knowledge of God. 6 For the Lord gives wisdom; From His mouth come knowledge and understanding; 7 He stores up sound wisdom for the upright; He is a shield to those who walk uprightly; 8 He guards the paths of justice, And preserves the way of His saints. 9 Then you will understand righteousness and justice, Equity and every good path. 10 When wisdom enters your heart, And knowledge is pleasant to your soul, 11 Discretion will preserve you; Understanding will keep you, 12 To deliver you from the way of evil, From the man who speaks perverse things, 13 From those who leave the paths of

AN EXPRESSION OF GOD'S WISDOM

DAY 21

uprightness To walk in the ways of darkness; 14 Who rejoice in doing evil, And delight in the perversity of the wicked; 15 Whose ways are crooked, And who are devious in their paths; 16 To deliver you from the immoral woman, From the seductress who flatters with her words, 17 Who forsakes the companion of her youth, And forgets the covenant of her God. 18 For her house [a]leads down to death, And her paths to the dead;19 None who go to her return, Nor do they [b]regain the paths of life— 20 So you may walk in the way of goodness, And keep to the paths of righteousness. 21 For the upright will dwell in the land, And the blameless will remain in it; 22 But the wicked will be [c]cut off from the [d] earth,And the unfaithful will be uprooted from it. **Proverbs 2 NKJV.**

PRAYER POINTS

1. Prayer of thanksgiving for being An Expression of God's Wisdom.
2. Prayer of greater insight and appreciation for being An Expression of God's Wisdom.
3. Decree by God's grace you are An Expression of God's Wisdom.

AFFIRMATION

I......... affirm, I am an Expression of God's Wisdom. I requested and trusted God for wisdom. He gave generously and did not deny me, for I asked in faith, and did not doubt. It is written "he who doubts is like a wave of the sea driven and tossed by the wind." I have inclined my ear to wisdom, and apply my heart to understanding; Yes, I cried out for discernment, and lifted up my voice for understanding. Wisdom is precious to me more than silver, and I have searched for her as for hidden treasures. By the grace of God, now I have access to Divine Wisdom. For it is written "the Lord gives wisdom; From His mouth come knowledge and understanding; He stores up sound wisdom for the upright; He is a shield to those who walk uprightly." the Lord Created, Redeemed and Sustained me in Wisdom. The life that I live now is no more my own. I am An Expression of God's Wisdom!

PART 4
OVERFLOW
Affirmations
DAILY PROPHETIC DECLARATIONS TO POSITION YOU FOR DIVINE OVERFLOW

DAY 22
AN INSTRUMENT OF GOD'S POWER

Scriptures for Reflection

12 He has made the earth by His power, He has established the world by His wisdom, And has stretched out the heavens at His discretion. 13 When He utters His voice, There is a [c]multitude of waters in the heavens: "And He causes the vapors to ascend from the ends of the earth. He makes lightning for the rain, He brings the wind out of His treasuries." 14 Everyone is dull-hearted, without knowledge; Every metalsmith is put to shame by an image; For his molded image is falsehood, And there is no breath in them. 15 They are futile, a work of errors; In the time of their punishment they shall perish. 16 The Portion of Jacob is not like them, For He is the Maker of all things, And Israel is the tribe of His inheritance; the Lord of hosts is His name. **Jeremiah 10:12-16 NKJV.**

the Lord builds up Jerusalem; He gathers together the outcasts of Israel. 3 He heals the brokenhearted And binds up their [b]wounds. 4 He counts the number of the stars; He calls them all by name. 5 Great is our Lord, and mighty in power; His understanding is infinite. 6 the Lord lifts up the humble; He casts the wicked down to the ground. **Psalms 147:2-6 NKJV.**

17 O God, You have taught me from my youth; And to this day I declare Your wondrous works. 18 Now also when I am old and grayheaded, O God, do not forsake me, Until I declare Your strength to this generation, Your power to everyone who is to come. **Psalms 71:17-18 NKJV.**

PRAYER POINTS

1. Prayer of thanksgiving for being an instrument of God's Power.
2. Prayer of greater insight and appreciation for being an instrument of God's Power.
3. Decree by God's grace you are an instrument of God's Power.

AFFIRMATION

I......... affirm, I am an instrument of God's Power. I have been made complete; achieving spiritual stature through Christ. He is the head over all rule and authority of every angelic and earthly power. I was buried with Him in baptism and raised with Him to a new life through my faith in the working of God, as displayed when He raised Christ from the dead. God made me alive together with Christ, having freely forgiven me all my sins and made me His righteousness in Christ. I am entrusted with the Holy Spirit. The power of the Most High is partnering with me to accomplish divine purposes on earth. By His divine power and sovereign will, God has given me everything I need for living a godly and Christ centred life. I have received all of this by intimacy with him, the one Who called me to Himself by means of His marvellous glory and excellence. I am an Instrument of God's Power to destroy the works of the devil. I am an Instrument of God's Power to establish His purposes on earth. I..... affirm, I am an instrument of God's Power!

A Carrier Of God's Glory

DAY 23

Scriptures for Reflection

Every king in all the earth will thank you, Lord, for all of them will hear your words. 5 Yes, they will sing about the Lord's ways, for the glory of the Lord is very great. **Psalm 138:4-5 NLT**. They were calling out to each other, "Holy, holy, holy is the LORD of Heaven's Armies! The whole earth is filled with his glory!" **Isaiah 6:3 NLT**.

16 The Spirit Himself bears witness with our spirit that we are children of God, 17 and if children, then heirs—heirs of God and joint heirs with Christ, if indeed we suffer with Him, that we may also be glorified together.

From Suffering to Glory

18 For I consider that the sufferings of this present time are not worthy to be compared with the glory which shall be revealed in us. **Romans 8:16-18 NKJV**.

Christ's Epistle

3 Do we begin again to commend ourselves? Or do we need, as some others, epistles of commendation to you or letters of commendation from you? 2 You are our epistle written in our hearts, known and read by all men; 3 clearly you are an epistle of Christ, ministered by us, written not with ink but by the Spirit of the living God, not on tablets of stone but on tablets of flesh, that is, of the heart.

The Spirit, Not the Letter.

4 And we have such trust through Christ toward God. 5 Not that we are sufficient of ourselves to think of anything as being from ourselves, but our sufficiency is from God, 6 who also made us sufficient as ministers of the new covenant, not of the letter but of the [a]Spirit; for the letter kills, but the Spirit gives life.

Glory of the New Covenant.

7 But if the ministry of death, written and engraved on stones, was glorious, so that the children of Israel could not look steadily at the face of Moses because of the glory of his countenance, which glory was passing away, 8 how will the ministry of the Spirit not be more glorious? 9 For if the ministry of condemnation had glory, the ministry of righteousness exceeds much more in glory. 10 For even what was made glorious had no glory in this respect, because of the glory that excels. 11 For if what is passing

DAY 23
A Carrier Of God's Glory

away was glorious, what remains is much more glorious. 12 Therefore, since we have such hope, we use great boldness of speech— 13 unlike Moses, who put a veil over his face so that the children of Israel could not look steadily at the end of what was passing away. 14 But their minds were blinded. For until this day the same veil remains unlifted in the reading of the Old Testament, because the veil is taken away in Christ. 15 But even to this day, when Moses is read, a veil lies on their heart. 16 Nevertheless when one turns to the Lord, the veil is taken away. 17 Now the Lord is the Spirit; and where the Spirit of the Lord is, there is liberty. 18 But we all, with unveiled face, beholding as in a mirror the glory of the Lord, are being transformed into the same image from glory to glory, just as [b]by the Spirit of the Lord. **2 Corinthians 3 NKJV.**

Prayer Points

1. Prayer of thanksgiving for being A Carrier of God's Glory.
2. Prayer of greater insight and appreciation for being A Carrier of God's Glory.
3. Decree by God's grace you are A Carrier of God's Glory.

AFFIRMATION

I......... affirm, I am A Carrier of God's Glory. God Created, Designed and Redeemed me for His Glory. Because I am born of God, that glory is inside me right now. All things that the Father has including His glory belongs to me. As a born again believer, it is my destiny to manifest God's glory here on earth. I declare the whole created order is filled with His glory. Even as the WORD became flesh and the glory was seen in Him as the begotten of The Father, so will I manifest my Father and my God's glory. I boldly declare I would know the hope of His calling, which is the hope of His glory. For the word declares, "For I consider that the sufferings of this present time are not worthy to be compared with the glory which shall be revealed in us." I understand through the revealed truth, that the God of my Lord Jesus Christ, the Father of glory, has given me the spirit of wisdom and revelation in the knowledge of Him, the eyes of my understanding are being enlightened day by day. I boldly proclaim I now know what the hope of His calling is. I have access through faith to the riches of the glory of His inheritance in the saints. I have the exceeding greatness of His power toward me who believes, according to the working of His mighty power which He worked in Christ when He raised Him from the dead and seated Him at His right hand in the heavenly places, far above all principality and power and might and dominion, and every name that is named, not only in this age but also in that which is to come. I affirm I am seated spiritually with Jesus right now in Heavenly places. On earth, I am A Carrier of God's Glory!

A Person Of Value — DAY 24

Scriptures for Reflection

O Lord, our Lord, How majestic and glorious and excellent is Your name in all the earth! You have displayed Your splendor above the heavens. 2 Out of the mouths of infants and nursing babes You have established strength Because of Your adversaries, That You might silence the enemy and make the revengeful cease. 3 When I see and consider Your heavens, the work of Your fingers, The moon and the stars, which You have established, 4 What is man that You are mindful of him, And the son of [earth-born] man that You care for him? 5 Yet You have made him a little lower than [b]God, And You have crowned him with glory and honor. 6 You made him to have dominion over the works of Your hands; You have put all things under his feet, 7 All sheep and oxen, And also the beasts of the field, 8 The birds of the air, and the fish of the sea, Whatever passes through the paths of the seas. 9 O Lord, our Lord, How majestic and glorious and excellent is Your name in all the earth! **Psalm 8 NKJV**

But Zion said, "the Lord has forsaken me, And my Lord has forgotten me." 15 "Can a woman forget her nursing child, [j]And not have compassion on the son of her womb? Surely they may forget, Yet I will not forget you. 16 See, I have inscribed you on the palms of My hands; Your walls are continually before Me. **Isaiah 49:14-16 NKJV**.

24 "A disciple is not above his teacher, nor a servant above his master. 25 It is enough for a disciple that he be like his teacher, and a servant like his master. If they have called the master of the house [g]Beelzebub, how much more will they call those of his household! 26 Therefore do not fear them. For there is nothing covered that will not be revealed, and hidden that will not be known.

Jesus Teaches the Fear of God

27 "Whatever I tell you in the dark, speak in the light; and what you hear in the ear, preach on the housetops. 28 And do not fear those who kill the body but cannot kill the soul. But rather fear Him who is able to destroy both soul and body in [h]hell. 29 Are not two sparrows sold for a [i]copper coin? And not one of them falls to the ground apart from your Father's will. 30 But the very hairs of your head are all numbered. 31 Do not fear therefore; you are of more value than many sparrows. Confess Christ Before Men.

32 "Therefore whoever confesses Me before men, him I will also confess before My Father who is in heaven. 33 But whoever denies Me before men, him I will also deny before My Father who is in heaven. **Matthew 10:24-32 NKJV**.

DAY 24
A Person Of Value

Prayer Points

1. Prayer of thanksgiving for being A Person of Value.
2. Pray for the grace and wisdom as A Person of Value you will be sensitive to your assignment and the cause of humanity.
3. Decree by God's grace you are A Person of Value.

AFFIRMATION

I......... affirm, I am A Person of Value. God created me in His image. Therefore, there is an Intrinsic Worth to me. I stand in solidarity for human Dignity. My life is sacred, so is my neighbour's. I declare from this day onwards I will live a life that is consistent with my human dignity. I am a gift from God to represent His interest on earth. I am A Person of Value.

DAY 25 A Custodian of the Spirit Empowered Boldness

Scriptures for Reflection

The wicked flee when no one pursues, But the righteous are bold as a lion. **Proverbs 28:1 NKJV.**

I will praise You with my whole heart; Before the gods I will sing praises to You. 2 I will worship toward Your holy temple, And praise Your name For Your lovingkindness and Your truth; For You have magnified Your word above all Your name. 3 In the day when I cried out, You answered me, And made me bold with strength in my soul. **Psalm 138:1-3 NKJV**

For truly against Your holy Servant Jesus, whom You anointed, both Herod and Pontius Pilate with the Gentiles and the people of Israel, were gathered together 28 to do whatever Your hand and Your purpose determined before to be done. 29 Now, Lord, look on their threats, and grant to Your servants that with all boldness they may speak Your word, 30 by stretching out Your hand to heal, and that signs and wonders may be done through the name of Your holy Servant Jesus." 31 And when they had prayed, the place where they were assembled together was shaken; and they were all filled with the Holy Spirit, and they spoke the word of God with boldness. **Acts 4:27-31 NKJV.**

Prayer Points

1. Prayer of thanksgiving for being A Custodian of the Spirit Empowered Boldness.
2. Pray for the grace and wisdom needed to walk in boldness. Decree you will be sensitive to your assignment and call and will not hold back.
3. Decree by God's grace you are As Bold as a lion.

AFFIRMATION

I......... affirm, I am A Custodian of the Spirit Empowered Boldness. My God has not given me the spirit of fear, but the spirit of boldness and sound mind. From this day onwards, I will pursue the Kingdom of God and its righteousness with uncommon boldness. Whatever it takes Lord, decrease the hold that unbelieving fear has over me and increase my boldness to declare the gospel to everyone you put in my path. I affirm as the righteousness of God in Christ, I am as bold as a lion. I am A Custodian of the Spirit Empowered Boldness!

An Anointed Vessel Unto the Lord

DAY 26

Scriptures for Reflection

"Make an altar of acacia wood for burning incense. 2 It is to be square, a cubit long and a cubit wide, and two cubits high[a]—its horns of one piece with it. 3 Overlay the top and all the sides and the horns with pure gold, and make a gold molding around it. 4 Make two gold rings for the altar below the molding—two on each of the opposite sides—to hold the poles used to carry it. 5 Make the poles of acacia wood and overlay them with gold. 6 Put the altar in front of the curtain that shields the ark of the covenant law—before the atonement cover that is over the tablets of the covenant law—where I will meet with you. 7 "Aaron must burn fragrant incense on the altar every morning when he tends the lamps. 8 He must burn incense again when he lights the lamps at twilight so incense will burn regularly before the Lord for the generations to come. 9 Do not offer on this altar any other incense or any burnt offering or grain offering, and do not pour a drink offering on it. 10 Once a year Aaron shall make atonement on its horns. This annual atonement must be made with the blood of the atoning sin offering[b] for the generations to come. It is most holy to the Lord."

Atonement Money

11 Then the Lord said to Moses, 12 "When you take a census of the Israelites to count them, each one must pay the Lord a ransom for his life at the time he is counted. Then no plague will come on them when you number them. 13 Each one who crosses over to those already counted is to give a half shekel,[c] according to the sanctuary shekel, which weighs twenty gerahs. This half shekel is an offering to the Lord. 14 All who cross over, those twenty years old or more, are to give an offering to the Lord. 15 The rich are not to give more than a half shekel and the poor are not to give less when you make the offering to the Lord to atone for your lives. 16 Receive the atonement money from the Israelites and use it for the service of the tent of meeting. It will be a memorial for the Israelites before the Lord, making atonement for your lives."

Basin for Washing.

17 Then the Lord said to Moses, 18 "Make a bronze basin, with its bronze stand, for washing. Place it between the tent of meeting and the altar, and put water in it. 19 Aaron and his sons are to wash their hands and feet with water from it. 20 Whenever they enter the tent of meeting, they shall wash with water so that they will not die. Also, when they approach the altar to minister by presenting a food offering to the Lord, 21 they shall wash their hands and feet so that they will not die. This is to be a lasting ordinance for Aaron and his descendants for the generations to come."

Anointing Oil.

DAY 26

AN ANOINTED VESSEL UNTO THE LORD

22 Then the Lord said to Moses, 23 "Take the following fine spices: 500 shekels[d] of liquid myrrh, half as much (that is, 250 shekels) of fragrant cinnamon, 250 shekels[e] of fragrant calamus, 24 500 shekels of cassia—all according to the sanctuary shekel—and a hin[f] of olive oil. 25 Make these into a sacred anointing oil, a fragrant blend, the work of a perfumer. It will be the sacred anointing oil. 26 Then use it to anoint the tent of meeting, the ark of the covenant law, 27 the table and all its articles, the lampstand and its accessories, the altar of incense, 28 the altar of burnt offering and all its utensils, and the basin with its stand. 29 You shall consecrate them so they will be most holy, and whatever touches them will be holy. 30 "Anoint Aaron and his sons and consecrate them so they may serve me as priests. 31 Say to the Israelites, 'This is to be my sacred anointing oil for the generations to come. 32 Do not pour it on anyone else's body and do not make any other oil using the same formula. It is sacred, and you are to consider it sacred. 33 Whoever makes perfume like it and puts it on anyone other than a priest must be cut off from their people.'"

Incense

34 Then the Lord said to Moses, "Take fragrant spices—gum resin, onycha and galbanum—and pure frankincense, all in equal amounts, 35 and make a fragrant blend of incense, the work of a perfumer. It is to be salted and pure and sacred. 36 Grind some of it to powder and place it in front of the ark of the covenant law in the tent of meeting, where I will meet with you. It shall be most holy to you. 37 Do not make any incense with this formula for yourselves; consider it holy to the Lord. 38 Whoever makes incense like it to enjoy its fragrance must be cut off from their people." **Exodus 30 NIV.**

The Parable of the Ten Virgins

25 "At that time the kingdom of heaven will be like ten virgins

who took their lamps and went out to meet the bridegroom. 2 Five of them were foolish and five were wise. 3 The foolish ones took their lamps but did not take any oil with them. 4 The wise ones, however, took oil in jars along with their lamps. 5 The bridegroom was a long time in coming, and they all became drowsy and fell asleep. 6 "At midnight the cry rang out: 'Here's the bridegroom! Come out to meet him!' 7 "Then all the virgins woke up and trimmed their lamps. 8 The foolish ones said to the wise, 'Give us some of your oil; our lamps are going out.' 9 "'No,' they replied, 'there may not be enough for both us and you. Instead, go to those who sell oil and buy some for yourselves.' 10 "But while they were on their way to buy the oil, the bridegroom arrived. The virgins who were ready went in with him to the wedding banquet. And the door was shut. 11 "Later the others also came. 'Lord, Lord,' they said, 'open the door for us!' 12 "But he replied, 'Truly I tell you, I don't know you.' 13 "Therefore keep watch, because you do not know the day or the hour. **Mathew 25:1-13 NKJV.**

Jesus Taken Up Into Heaven

1. In my former book, Theophilus, I wrote about all that Jesus began to do and to teach 2 until the day he was taken up to heaven, after giving instructions through the Holy Spirit to the apostles he had chosen. 3 After his suffering, he presented himself to them and gave many convincing proofs that he was alive. He appeared to them over a period of forty days and spoke about the kingdom of God. 4 On one occasion, while he was eating with them, he gave them this command: "Do not leave Jerusalem, but wait for the gift my Father promised, which you have heard me speak about. 5 For John baptized with[a] water, but in a few days you will be baptized with[b] the Holy Spirit." 6 Then they gathered around him and asked him, "Lord, are you at this time going to restore the kingdom to Israel?" 7 He said to them: "It is not for you to know the times or dates the Father has set by his own authority. 8 But you will receive power when the Holy Spirit comes on you; and you will be my witnesses in Jerusalem, and in all Judea and Samaria, and to the ends of the earth." Acts 1:1-8 NIV.

DAY 26
AN ANOINTED VESSEL UNTO THE LORD

PRAYER POINTS

1. Prayer of thanksgiving for being An Anointed Vessel unto the Lord.
2. Pray for the grace and wisdom needed to be a faithful witness about the Lord Jesus.
3. Decree by God's grace you are An Anointed Vessel unto the Lord.

AFFIRMATION

I......... affirm, I am An Anointed Vessel unto the Lord. My God Has exalted my horn like that of the wild ox, oh yes I have been anointed with fresh oil. Now let it be known, I have an anointing from the Holy One, and my spirit deep within me is empowered to know all things. The unction which I have received from Jesus abides in me. I have been anointed with the oil of gladness, my cup is overflowing with unspeakable joy. The life that I live now is for the benefit of witnessing about my Lord and Master Jesus. I am An Anointed Vessel unto the Lord.

DAY 27 A RECEPIENT OF THE PEACE OF GOD

Scriptures for Reflection

You will keep him in perfect peace, Whose mind is stayed on You, Because he trusts in You. 4 Trust in the Lord forever, For in Yah, the Lord, is [b]everlasting strength...... 12 Lord, You will establish peace for us, For You have also done all our works [g]in us. **Isaiah 26:3-4, 12 NKJV.**

"For this is like the waters of Noah to Me; For as I have sworn That the waters of Noah would no longer cover the earth, So have I sworn That I would not be angry with you, nor rebuke you. 10 For the mountains shall depart And the hills be removed, But My kindness shall not depart from you, Nor shall My covenant of peace be removed," Says the Lord, who has mercy on you. **Isaiah 54:9-10 NKJV.**

6 Be anxious for nothing, but in everything by prayer and supplication, with thanksgiving, let your requests be made known to God; 7 And the peace of God, which transcends all understanding, will guard your hearts and your minds in Christ Jesus. 8 Finally, brothers and sisters, whatever is true, whatever is noble, whatever is right, whatever is pure, whatever is lovely, whatever is admirable—if anything is excellent or praiseworthy—think about such things. 9 Whatever you have learned or received or heard from me, or seen in me—put it into practice. And the God of peace will be with you. **Philippians 4:6-9. NKJV**

PRAYER POINTS

1. Prayer of thanksgiving for being A Recipient of the Peace of God.
2. Pray for the grace and wisdom needed to be a faithful witness about the Lord Jesus.
3. Decree by God's grace you are An Anointed Vessel unto the Lord.

AFFIRMATION

I......... affirm, I am A Recipient of the Peace of God. I have a tranquil state of appreciation and faith as I have submitted to and trusted in the LORD with all my heart and leaned not on my own understanding. The God of peace Himself, has sanctified me through and through. My whole spirit, soul and body is kept blameless for I have peace with God through the blood of Jesus. I am convinced that neither death nor life, neither angels nor demons, neither the present nor the future, nor any powers, neither height nor depth, nor anything else in all creation, will be able to separate me from the love of God that is in Christ Jesus my Lord. I am A Recipient of the Peace of God!

A Beneficiary Of The Light Of God's Countenance — DAY 28

Scriptures for Reflection

22 And the Lord spoke to Moses, saying: 23 "Speak to Aaron and his sons, saying, 'This is the way you shall bless the children of Israel. Say to them: 24 "the Lord bless you and keep you; 25 the Lord make His face shine upon you, And be gracious to you; 26 the Lord [e]lift up His countenance upon you, And give you peace." 27 "So they shall [f]put My name on the children of Israel, and I will bless them." **Numbers 6:22-27 NKJV**

7 For the Lord is righteous, He loves righteousness; [c]His countenance beholds the upright. **Psalm 11:7 NKJV.**

15 My times are in Your hand; Deliver me from the hand of my enemies, And from those who persecute me. 16 Make Your face shine upon Your servant; Save me for Your mercies' sake. **Psalm 31:15-16 NKJV.**

righteousness and justice are the foundation of Your throne; Mercy and truth go before Your face. 15 Blessed are the people who know the joyful sound! They walk, O Lord, in the light of Your countenance. 16 In Your name they rejoice all day long, And in Your righteousness they are exalted. 17 For You are the glory of their strength, And in Your favor our [c]horn is exalted. **Psalm 89:14-17 NKJV**

Prayer Points

1. Prayer of thanksgiving for being A Beneficiary Of The Light Of God's Countenance.
2. Pray for the grace and wisdom needed to be a faithful Beneficiary Of The Light Of God's Countenance.
3. Decree by God's grace you are A responsible Beneficiary Of The Light Of God's Countenance

AFFIRMATION

I......... affirm, I am A Beneficiary Of The Light of His Countenance. I declare righteousness and justice are the foundation of God's throne. Mercy and truth go before Him forever and ever. I am Blessed for I know the joyful sound of my God! I walk, O Lord, in the light of Your countenance. In Your name I rejoice all day long, And in Your righteousness I am exalted. For You are the glory of of my strength, And in Your favor my horn is exalted. I am A Beneficiary The Light of God's Countenance.

DAY 29 A LIVING TEMPLE OF GOD

Scriptures for Reflection

Then the word of the Lord came to me, saying: 10 "Receive the gift from the captives—from Heldai, Tobijah, and Jedaiah, who have come from Babylon—and go the same day and enter the house of Josiah the son of Zephaniah. 11 Take the silver and gold, make an[b] elaborate crown, and set it on the head of Joshua the son of Jehozadak, the high priest. 12 Then speak to him, saying, 'Thus says the Lord of hosts, saying: "Behold, the Man whose name is the BRANCH! From His place He shall [c]branch out, And He shall build the temple of the Lord; 13 Yes, He shall build the temple of the Lord. He shall bear the glory, And shall sit and rule on His throne; So He shall be a priest on His throne, And the counsel of peace shall be between [d]them both." **Zachariah 6:9-13 NKJV.**

9 For we are God's fellow workers; you are God's field, you are God's building. 10 According to the grace of God which was given to me, as a wise master builder I have laid the foundation, and another builds on it. But let each one take heed how he builds on it. 11 For no other foundation can anyone lay than that which is laid, which is Jesus Christ. 12 Now if anyone builds on this foundation with gold, silver, precious stones, wood, hay, straw, 13 each one's work will become clear; for the Day will declare it, because it will be revealed by fire; and the fire will test each one's work, of what sort it is. 14 If anyone's work which he has built on it endures, he will receive a reward. 15 If anyone's work is burned, he will suffer loss; but he himself will be saved, yet so as through fire. 16 Do you not know that you are the temple of God and that the Spirit of God dwells in you? 17 If anyone [b]defiles the temple of God, God will destroy him. For the temple of God is holy, which temple you are. **1 Corinthians 3:9-17 NKJV**

15 Do you not know that your bodies are members of Christ? Shall I then take the members of Christ and make them members of a harlot? Certainly not! 16 Or do you not know that he who is joined to a harlot is one body with her? For "the two," He says, "shall become one flesh." 17 But he who is joined to the Lord is one spirit with Him. **1 Corinthians 6:15-16 NKJV.**

A Living Temple Of God
DAY 29

Prayer Points

1. Prayer of thanksgiving for being A Living Temple of God.
2. Pray for the grace and wisdom needed to be A Holy Temple of God.
3. Decree by God's grace you are A Living Temple of God.

AFFIRMATION

I......... affirm, I am A Living Temple of God. As a believer in Jesus, I am His temple, because I have been separated from idolatry and impurity, and consecrated to sacred purposes, and have been dedicated to the honour of Him whom I worship. I am a living temple because I have been redeemed to offer up to Him dutiful worship and acceptable sacrifices. Not sacrifices of appeasement, but daily spiritual sacrifices acceptable for the mercies of God, and the blessings of His great salvation. Every faculty and affection of my redeemed soul is engaged in the service as a living temple. As a believer in Christ, I am a living temple of my God, because He inhabits in me to manifest His glory in and through me. I am A Living Temple of God.

DAY 30
Salt Covenant

Scriptures for Reflection

Then Abijah stood on Mount Zemaraim, which is in the mountains of Ephraim, and said, "Hear me, Jeroboam and all Israel: 5 Should you not know that the Lord God of Israel gave the dominion over Israel to David forever, to him and his sons, by a covenant of salt? **2 Chronicles 13:4-5 NKJV**

And every offering of your grain offering you shall season with salt; you shall not allow the salt of the covenant of your God to be lacking from your grain offering. With all your offerings you shall offer salt. **Leviticus 2:13 NKJV**

All the heave offerings of the holy things, which the children of Israel offer to the Lord, I have given to you and your sons and daughters with you as an ordinance forever; it is a covenant of salt forever before the Lord with you and your descendants with you." **Numbers 18:19 NKJV**

5 Walk in wisdom toward those who are outside, redeeming the time. 6 Let your speech always be with grace, seasoned with salt, that you may know how you ought to answer each one. **Colossians 4:5-6 NKJV.**

49 "For everyone will be seasoned with fire, and[p] every sacrifice will be seasoned with salt. 50 Salt is good, but if the salt loses its flavor, how will you season it? Have salt in yourselves, and have peace with one another." **Mark 9:49-50 NKJV.**

13 "You are the salt of the earth; but if the salt loses its flavor, how shall it be seasoned? It is then good for nothing but to be thrown out and trampled underfoot by men. **Matthew 5:13**

PRAYER POINTS

1. Prayer of thanksgiving for being The Salt of The Earth.
2. Pray for the grace and wisdom needed to Preserve, Flavour and Communalise.
3. Decree by God's grace you are The Salt of The Earth.

AFFIRMATION

I.......... affirm, I am The Salt of The Earth. God's flavour and preservative agent to my family and the world around me. I'm walking in wisdom, redeeming the time. I am God's instrument of grace interceding for the world around me. I am a good flavour of God to my family. I am The Salt of The Earth.

About The Author

Richard Amoaye is the founder of Inspiring Greatness. He believes that trapped within every person is the seed of greatness, and he is on a mission to help people discover and nurture their God given potential. It was in Sydney that he learnt God had given him a mandate to Raise Champions through God's Power for Kingdom Advancement.

This mandate led him on a journey that birthed God's Power Ministries (GPM), a dynamic apostolic and prophetic ministry which he pioneered in 2010 alongside his wife Reverend Patrice Amoaye. The diverse and vibrant multi-site ministry is headquartered in Sydney Australia. Not long after, Inspiring Greatness was also born!

A prophet by call, Richard's love for God knows no bounds and it propels him to serve in different capacities. He preaches, teaches, mentors and writes, all done with one goal in mind – to empower people from all walks of life. He provides wise counsel, is a consultant and advisor to many including leaders in ministry and the marketplace.

Outside of ministry, the husband and father of two finds joy in spending quality time with his family. He is an avid reader and now, a prolific writer. He is the author of Decoding the Mystery of Excellence, a 31-day devotional titled 'Joy comes in the Morning', Power for Exploits and The Excellence of Wisdom in addition to a mini book on prayer and a reflection series on wisdom. He also wrote 'Not Perfect', a deeply reflective song on God's love that is featured on the Greater Grace Power Worship Album.

Books By Richard Amoaye

Power for Exploits

The Excellence of Wisdom

My Secret Place:
Inspired thoughts and Scriptures for daily living
Volumes 1, 2 and 3

Unveiling the heart of prayer

Joy comes in the Morning:
31 days of living in the fullness of Joy in all Circumstances
(Devotional)

Decoding The Mystery Of Excellence

To Contact the Author:
Email: **info@richardamoayeministries.com**
Visit: **www.amoaye.org**

www.ingramcontent.com/pod-product-compliance
Lightning Source LLC
Chambersburg PA
CBHW040243010526
44107CB00065B/2859